TAJ MA

AGRA & FATEHPUR SIKRI

age
Greenage
Books

MAP OF TAJ MAHAL

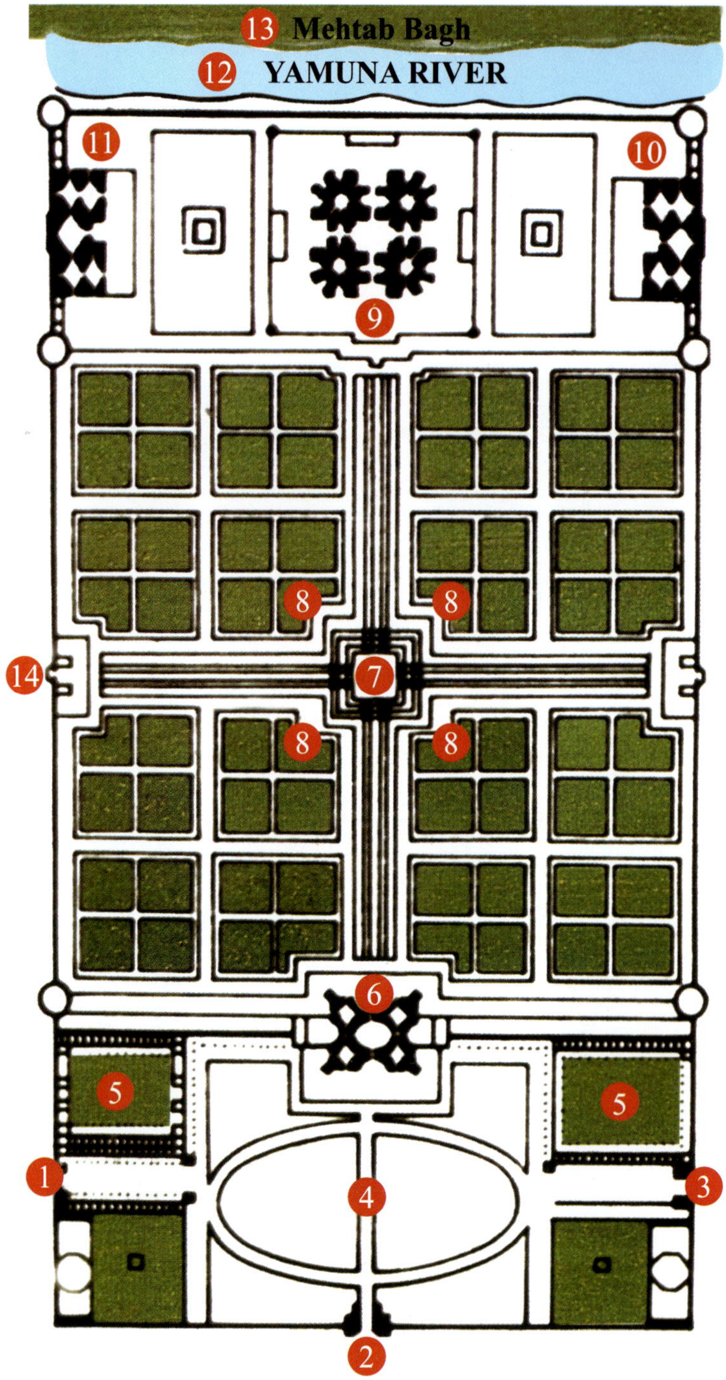

1 WEST GATE (ENTRANCE)
2 SEEDI GATE (ENTRANCE)
3 EAST GATE (ENTRANCE)
4 FORE COURT
5 SERVANTS QUARTER
6 MAIN GATE
7 ORNAMENTAL POOL
8 CHAR BAGH
9 TOMB
10 GUEST HOUSE
11 MOSQUE
12 YAMUNA RIVER
13 MEHTAB BAGH
14 MUSEUM

AGRA

Dream In Marble

The history of Agra before the Muslim conquest is shrouded in obscurity. The only reference to it is one by the Persian poet, Salman, who died in 1131, A.D. It is stated that Mahmud so ruined Agra, which had been a great Hindu strong hold since the days of Kans, that it did not recover. In the great epic, Mahabharat, there is a reference to Agraban and this may well be Agra.

Sikandar Lodi who made Agra his capital in the year 1501 A.D. built a fort and laid out a city. He rebuilt his new capital after it was destroyed by an earthquake within a year of its foundation. Though none of the buildings in the city can be assigned to him, his name is preserved in the suburb of Sikandra, where he erected a baradari which is still standing. It was after his death that Babar, the first of the Great Mughals, continued to live at Agra and made it a city of gardens. Ram Bagh and Zohra Bagh are all that remain today.

Agra rose to prominence during the reign of Akbar. He built the Fort and made Agra the seat of one of the mightiest and richest kingdoms. From the years 1570 to 1585, he shifted his capital to Fatehepur Sikri, now a deserted city lying twenty seven miles south-west of Agra. It was, however, in the seventeenth century, during the reign of Shah Jahan, grandson of Akbar, that

Agra reached the peak of its glory as the city of immortal architecture. This period found expression in a style of architecture of exceptional splendour carried to the highest degree of perfection. Shah Jahan built much of the Fort, most the buildings of the city and the Taj—it was an age of marble culminating in its excellence in the Taj Mahal. Sandstone was replaced by marble in its most refined form. Shah Jahan resided here from 1632 to 1637 and renamed the city Akbarabad. The name however did not endure. It was here in Agra Fort that Shah Jahan was imprisoned by his son, Aurangzed, in 1658 for seven year. One may still see the prism which reflected the Taj and Thus lightened the last years of its builder.

BABUR
(1526-1530)

HUMAYUN
(1530-1556)

AKBAR
(1556-1605)

MUGHALS

Many stories of India's enormous wealth had spread far and wide. India was well- known as 'sone ki chidiya'. It had in its treasure, valuable precious and semi-precious stones. It was so famous that Timur came here and plundered almost all the wealth and he also took the finest craftsmen to beautify his capital 'Samarkand'.

The mughal empire was founded by Babur in India. He was so motivated to see India by an old woman who had narrated to him many stories about India, that he invaded India for four times but was unsuccessful and he succeeded in his fifth attempt. He found nothing that could interest him

After his death on 25 December 1530, Humayun ascended the throne. He was defeated by Sher Shah and he fled to Sind and in Umarkot Akbar was born , who ascended the throne in 1556 at the age of thirteen. Bairam Khan was his guardian at that time.

After some time he took over the whole charge . He had many learned men and ministers in his durbar one of the most important ministers was Birbal. Akbar had over 300 wives but was not enough lucky to have a son. To fulfill his wish of having a son he went to seek the blessings of Sheikh Saleem Chisti, a famous saint who resided in Sikri near Agra. He had a baby boy.

Whom he named Salim, later who was known as Jahangir. Akbar built Fatehpur Sikri in honour of the saint. Jahangir became a great scholar of Hindi, Arabian, Turkish and Persian. He got married to Noor Jahan.

In his later days he became addicted to women and wine. He died in 1628 and Shah Jahan ascended the throne. He was fond of building palaces and huge monuments. 'Taj' being the best of his construction is known worldwide. Shah Jahan's old age passed in agony and disgust due to his son Aurangzeb who destroyed the temples and tried to impose Islam on all the people of of his kingdom.

There are many a reasons for the down fall of the mighty Mughal Empire. The mighty empire , which was founded by Babur, and strengthened by the wit and wisdom of Akbar, the great, the same empire which was given the sense of justice by Jahangir and lustre and fashion of Noor Jahan which was immortalised by Shah Jahan by constructing the Taj Mahal, could not be retained by the unwisely and intolerant policy of Aurangzeb. All the successors of Aurangzeb were incompetent. Aurangzeb wanted to divide his kingdom amongst his three sons. But like a tradition of Mughal family, all the three started a struggle for the throne, ultimately, Prince Muajjam defeated the remaining two brothers in 1707 A.D. and he ascended the throne with the title of Bahadur Shah. But after a short spell of only five years, he died in Lahore in the year 712A.D.

During the later Mughals, there were so many incompetent successors in the Mughal Dynasty, that one after the other, were crowned and decrowned , even by their petty court nobles like Saiyyad Brothers until 1857A.D.Thus, the Mughal rulers ruled India for name only upto 1857 when ultimately they were routed by the British from the throne.

JAHANGIR
(1605-1628)

SHAH JAHAN
(1628-1658)

AURANGZEB
(1658-1707)

TAJ MAHAL

SUN RISE TO SUN SET • FRIDAY CLOSED • CHILD UPTO 15 YEARS FREE

Taj aptly called a 'dream in marble' is situated on the right banks of the Yamuna river. It is towards the South of the city and is at a distance of about three kms. The Taj Mahal, the most beautiful building of the world, is made of white marble, in the loving memory of the then Empress of India-named Arjumand Bano Begum. She was the grand daughter of Mirza Giyas Beg-who was later known as Itmad-ud-Daula and who was father of Noor Jahan, the wife of Prince Salim or Jahangir. The name of her father was Khwaja Abul Hasan entitled as Yamin-ud-Daula. Asaf Khan, who was real brother of Noor Jahan and was the Prime Minister of Jahangir's court. She was Persian by blood and was born on6thApril 1593 A.D. (14 Rajab 1001). She was very beautiful-like Noor Jahan, from her early childhood, and was liked by Noor Jahan very much. Her father arranged for her education in a royal manner and she developed in her all the qualities and merits of a royal family. When she became young, she attracted Prince Khurram and both of them started loving each other.

Shah Jahan and Mumtaz Mahal were inseparable lovers and it is clear from the incident that when Shah Jahan had to go to suppress a rebellion of Khan-e-Jahan Lodi at Burhanpur in the Deccan, then Mumtaz was also at the side of Shah Jahan in Burhanpur in that compaign. At the same time she gave birth to their fourteenth child, Gauhar Ara Begum, and fell seriously ill, It is said that at the time of her death, Mumtaz Mahal expressed her last wish to the Royal Emperor Shah Jahan that he will build a beautiful and incomparable monument over her grave as a token of their worldly inseparable love.

After the death of Mumtaz Mahal—'The Lady of the Taj', Shah Jahan could not bear this great loss of his dear wife and his health began to decline. For complete two years, he abstained himself from all kinds of pleasures and functions. On each Friday, Shah Jahan used to go to her grave on foot in white dress, to read 'Fatiha', accompanied by his courtiers and nobles.

The mortal remains of Mumtaz Mahal were given a temporary burial (Amanat) in the building which was situated inside a garden at Zainabad,

G-EAOU

opposite of Burhanpur on the other side of the River tapti in the month of June 1631. On 15th of June, 1631 (on Thursday, 25 Dhu'l-Qa'da 1040), the Emperor crossed River Tapti and went to the grave and shed oceans of tears on her grave. He read 'Fatiha' prayers and on his return, distributed alms etc. for the heavenly peace of the departed soul. On 1st December, 1631 A.D. (17 Jumada J, 1041), the dead body was sent to Agra, accompanied by various V.I.R's like Prince Shuja, Nawab Wazir Khan and the most beloved friend-cum secretary of Mumtaz Mahal, Sittiu'-Nisa Khanam. All along this journey, alms in cash, food and clothes were distributed freely to the poor as per Shah Jahan's wishes. The site, which was selected for the permanent grave of the queen, was a lofty mansion of Raja Jai Singh of Jaipur, situated towards the South of the city. As per Islamic religious rules, he was granted some other lofty residence in exchange. The dead body reached Agra on 29th December, 1631 A.D. (15 Jumada II 1041), and was again buried temporarily, under a temporary stracuure in the north-west corner of the garden on the bank of river Jamuna. The Emperor announced a memorial to be built for his dear wife and invited designs from the famous architects of the world. So many designs were put before the emperor, but ultimately the design of Ustad Isa Afandi of Turkey was selected and the construction of the Taj started.

The main building material, the white marble of top quality, was brought from Makrana, a well-known place in the Nagaur District of Rajasthan.

The other material such as Red stone, was brought from Dholpur and Fatehpur Sikri. The yellow and black marble was brought from Narbads and Charkoh respectively. Some precious stones, gold and silver were received from various kings and chiefs of the empire and from abroad. Besides all these materials, some other materials were brought from far off lands.

The construction work started in the month of December, 1631 A.D. and it came to a finish in the year 1648. The completion of it took twenty two years to build and some twenty thousand laborers worked on it. After the construction of the main building, the other buildings surrounding the Taj and the Taj Garden's were taken up. Not only this, but some adjacent buildings were also erected in which the Mosque towards the west, another building named Jamat Khana towards the east, a big boundary like huge

platform towards river Jamuna and a very big three storeyed entrance gate took another five years. Further the Mosque in the front and some other smaller buildings took another five years. Thus, in total, the Taj took 22 long years in its completion. It is said that twenty two small domes on the main entrance gate of the Taj represent twenty two years spent in the construction of the Taj.

On the occasion of the first anniversary of Mumtaj Mahal, Shah Jahan ordered for an 'Urs' to be celebrated. As per the orders of the Emperor, the attendants of the house hold, setup some huge and lofty tents with golden strings and curtains alongwith costly carpets. The emperor himself, the court nobles, mansabdars, the leading personalities of the city, the holy people, the learned ones, the "Huffaz"—those who knew the quran by heart.

The ladies of the house and an envoy from Iran, attended the 'Urs' and read Fatiha for the forgiveness of the departed soul. A beautiful feast was organised for the assembly with betels and scents. Out of Rs. one lakh, which was put a part for charitable deeds, about 50.000/- was spent in distributing the alms to the poor and the needy. At the conclusion of this 'Urs' all the lady members of the royal family along with other elite ladies, went round the grave of Mumtaz and held a meeting. The remaining sum of Rs.50,000/- was distributed as alms to the needy pious and the deserving females.

The southern Gate is towards the South, which faces the old Mumtazabad (Modern Taj Ganj). It is meant for the pedestrians or the pedlars only. On the right side of this gate is a Tomb of red stone which is surrounded by court Yards and crowned with a dome. It is said that there is a grave of one lady companion of Mumtaj Mahal. Due to this reason this building is called as the tomb of a Maid of Honour.

Eastern Gate faces towards Fatehabad. There is a domed tomb erected on an elevated platform near this gate. This tomb was built in the memory of another wife of Shah Jahan called Sirhindi Begum. Due to this, the gate is known as 'Sirhi Darwaza.' The main building is eight sided, having twenty four arches, a big hall and a verandah.

The Western Gate is the main entrance of the Taj Mahal and this gate faces

towards the Agra cantonment and Agra city. There is a red sand stoneedifice outside this gate which is known as Fatehpuri Maszid, which was constructed in the memory of Fatehpuri Begum another wife of Shah Jahan. It is erected on a beautiful terrace.

After entering the huge gate, there is a beautiful tomb of Situ-nu-Nisa Khanam on the left side. She was the personal and favourite maid companion of Mumtaz Mahal. She was also the governess of Jahan Ara Begum the beloved daughter of Shah Jahan, who spent her days and lonely nights with her father. Situ-nu-Nisa was a childless widow and after the death of Mumtaz Mahal, she had gone to Lahore. She died in the year 1648 A.D. in Lahore and after her death, her body was brought to Agra in 1749 A.D. to be buried in the Taj complex as per the last wish of Mumtaz. The tomb is beautifully paved with marble. In the centre hall of this dome, the grave of Situ-un-Nisa is situated with beautiful and colourful paintings on the wall and the ceiling.

The Gate Way of Taj is an octagonal entrance hall, surrounded by small rooms on both the sides in the floors having beautifully ornamented gates on two sides, one opening towards the court yard side and the other to wards the Mausoleum itself. On the three sides of this gateway, there are strong balconies. The gate is a master piece of fine inlay work in itself. The profuse in lay work of white marble and precious stones into the red sandstone surface, has elegantly executed inscriptions in 'Thulth' script, inlayed with black marble on white marble surface, gives a charming look to the whole structure. Some Quranic texts are nicely inscribed in black letters. These Quranic verses do not appear bigger at the bottom then they are at the top. On the top there is a row of white marble cupolas and the corners are crowned by open domed kiosks.

Taj Gardens were designed by Ali Mardan Khan, who was a noble in the Mughal court.

Fountains and running channels of water with large reservoirs are typical of their garden designs. Water was drawn up from the river Jamuna by a system of buckets, dipping into the river and conveying water up by a chain way, drawn by the bullocks or by camel power. The river water was collected in some big reservoirs on the top of the rooms situated in the middle of the garden walls on both the sides of the Taj enclosure. From these artificial

reservoirs on the walls, water was taken through iron pipes to the fountains and the running water channels.

The tombs or graves of the Empress Mumtaz Mahal and Emperor Shah Jahan, are situated in the centric below the main dome.

Around the cenotaphs, there is a beautiful screen on rather an enclosure of eight sides, 6.25 feet high and each side of the screen being 12.5 feet in length. The emperor employed Saida of Gilam entitled Bibadal Khan, who was in the royal service as the Chief of the Goldsmith Establishment of Shah Jahan. He prepared a railing of gold with inscriptions, cupping-horns and floral designs worked in rare enamel, in which 40,000 tolas of gold was used. Likewise, a covering of pearl-strings worth several lakhs of rupees, used to be placed over the grave of Mumtaz Mahal on every Friday or on her death anniversary day.

The Taj is a perfect fusion of Indian and Persian architecture. It is worth mentioning here that Ustad Isa and his pupil Ustad Ahmad Paras were of Persian origin but both of them were Indian at the same time as they were converted to Islam. Thus it may be said that the exterior of the Taj is Persian yet the soul in it is, Indian. It is an established act that the designers and architects of the Taj were knowing Hindu Shilpa-Shastra.

It is a historical well-known fact, that the Mughal Emperors were under Hindu influence as had established matrimonial relations with the Hindus. The mothers of Jahangir, Jodhabai and that of Shah Jahan, was the daughter of Raja Udai Singh of Marwar. Thus the imperial mothers had a full influence upon their children-the future emperors of India. Taj Mahal, with its four corner minarets and the main building in the middle, is of the 'Panch-Prasada' type, and is purely Indian.

"For every hour of the day and for every atmospheric condition the Taj has its own colour values, from the soft dreaminess at dawn, and the dazzling whiteness at midday to its cold splendour in the moonlight, when the dome, thin of substance as the air, hangs, among the stars like a great pearl. Yet none of these effects can equal those few fleeting moments when, softly illuminated by the brief Indian after glow, it assumes the enchanting tint of some pale and lively rose."

AGRA FORT

SUNRISE TO SUNSET • CHILD UPTO 15 YEARS FREE

Apart from the Taj Mahal, Agra has yet another important place to visit. It is the famous fort of Agra, constructed by the Mighty Mughal Emperor, Akbar the Great. It is an amalgamation of buildings and palaces, which were built by Akbar, Jahangir, Shah Jahan and even Aurangzeb. Thus, it is a vast museum of building of various tastes and natures of the Mughal rulers.

Agra Fort is situated on the right bank of river Jamuna towards the east of Agra City. It has been built by thick and strong walls of red sand stone. It is said, that Akbar constructed this fort in place of the old Badalgarh Fort, which was a strong foothold of the Rajput rulers The Fort at Agra was surrounded by two big ditches. Out of these two, the inner ditch is still there while the outer ditch has been filled and there exist a road in place of it. Both the ditches were full of dread-ed crocodiles and tortoise so that the enemy may not cross them easily. This fort was started in 1565 A.D. and took eight long years in its completion. The construction was entrusted to Kashim Khan who was Akbar's commander in Chief and the Governor of Kabul,

After the down fall of the mighty Mughal Empire, this fort of Agra, had to bear upon some grievous hurts on its chest. First of all it had to bear the pangs in 1639 A.D. when Nadir Shah invaded and de-stroyed many of its parts. After that it faced the mighty Marathas and the Jats, while the later ones filled husk 'Bhusa' in the Taj and the Mughal buildings, ultimately, it had to face the anger of the Mutineers in 1857, when the Europeans had taken shelter in it to save their lives from the Mutineers and the patriotic public of Agra, Though this fort has lost that glamour and grandeur of the Mughal rule, yet it deserves a keen observation by the visitors. Previously Agra Fort had 4 main gates but now only the famous Amar singh Gate and the Delhi Gate are in use. The rest of the two gates-namely the water gate and the Darshani Gate or Darwaze have been closed permanently.

On the southern extremity of the fort, is Amar Singh Gate opened for the general public. This gate was built by Emperor Shah Jahan after the name of the great Rajput hero, Amar Singh Rathore, Maharaja of Jodhpur. It is

MAP OF THE AGRA FORT

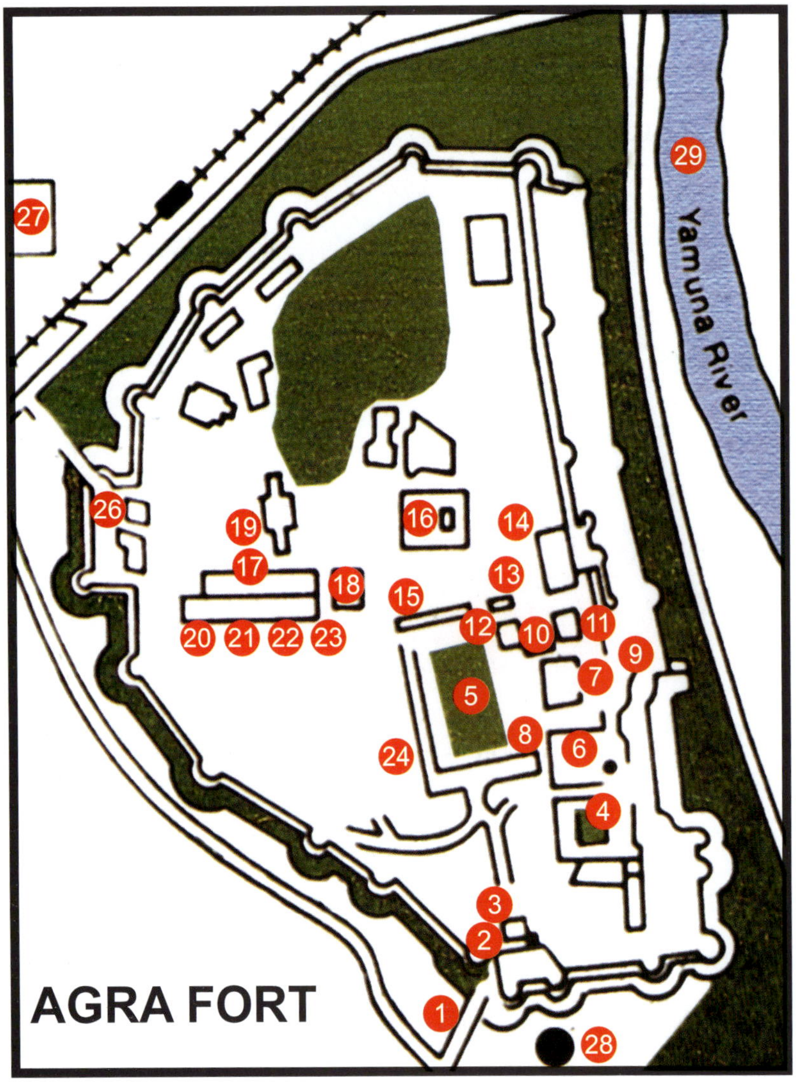

1. AMAR SINGH GATE
2. WATER GATE
3. DARSHINI GATE
4. JAHANGIR'S PALACE
5. GRAPE GARDEN
6. KHAS MAHAL
7. GOLDEN PAVILION
8. SHEESH MAHAL
9. MUSAMMAN BURJ
10. DIWAN-E-KHAS
11. KALA (BLACK) TAKHT
12. SAFED (WHITE) TAKHT
13. NAGEENA MASJID
14. MEENA MOSQUE
15. MACCHI BHAWAN
16. DIWAN-E-AAM
17. LADIES BAZAAR
18. MOTI MASJID
19. TAHKHANA
20. AKBARI MAHAL
21. SHAHJAHANI MAHAL
22. SALIM GARH
23. KURSI (CHAIR)
24. BAOLI
25. INLAY WORK
26. DELHI GATE
27. JAMI MASJID
28. SHIVAJI SMARAK
29. YAMUNA RIVER

said that in 1644 A.D. in full court of Emperor Shah Jahan, Salabat Khan, the imperial treasurer insulted him on which Amar Singh slew Salabat Khan. This turned the mughal army against Amar Singh. Riding on his horse back, he jumped of the high walls of the fort near the spot where now is built Amar Singh Gate. His sincere horse was half in the ditch and half on the road and died at once. In memory of this marvelous incident a horse in red sandstone was built.

Jahangir's Palace is a double storied building of red sand stone which is believed to be built by Akbar the Great for his son. Its walls and ceiling were painted with bright colours including golden paint in Rajput style. Later on, this edifice was built by Emperor Jahangir after demolishing one of the palace built by Akbar for his Hindu wife Jodha Bai.

Its all four sides had their separate utility, the western side as a personal Temple, a conversation hall in the North and a drawing room in the southern side. This palace was famous for its blend of Hindu and central Asian architectural styles. The Hindu Temple was destroyed by Emperor Aurangzeb.

Angoori Bagh is situated infront of the Khas Mahal. It was established by Akbar the Great for his empress and other ladies of his 'Harem'. It is said that the soil for this was brought from Kashmir. The garden is surrounded by double storied building on three sides.

Khas Mahal is a beautiful white marble structure. It was used as a 'Harem' by the ladies of the Royal Family and was called as 'Aram Gah' also. It was used as a drawing and sleeping room by Shah Jahan.

Diwan-i-Khas, the 'Hall of private and dignified Audience', was built by Shah Jahan, with white marble in the year 1637 A.D., which was towards the river side. It consists of two big halls. The pillars and arches of this dignified building are inlaid with semi precious stones and coloured flowers. Its ceiling was decorated with golden colours and the floors with shining marble slabs which were taken away by the Jats during their occupation of Agra. It is said, that this building too was made by the same artisans, who mode the Taj Mahal.

Diwan-i-Khas was the place where Royal Durbars or meetings were held in which the Mughal Emperor had some important confidential matters with

his Ministers and the Ambassadors of the court.

The famous peacock throne of Shah Jahan was placed here. Later it was taken to Delhi by Aurangzeb and later on it was taken away by the invaders, and is now present in Tehran.

Sheesh Mahal was used as a dressing room by the ladies of the 'Harem' and its walls are in laid with beautiful small mirrors. It is situated towards the north of Khas Mahal. It was built by Shah Jahan in 1630 A.D. in the form of a Turkish Bath for the use of his family members. It consists of two halls and two tanks, the one for hot water and the other for cold water. These chambers were paved with marble floors carved and in laid with designs offish. In the twilight of small and tiny lamps, reflecting their beams all round, the Mughal Emperor used to enjoy himself with many of his beautiful wives. The fountains were played with scented water rolling on the floors. This place was as a heaven on earth where beauty, charm and sex were cultured freely, but for the rulers only.

Jasmine Tower, Samman Burj, or Musamman Burj or octagonal Tower is one and the same building, which was built by Jahangir for his Empress Noor Jahan. Later on it was remodeled by Shah Jahan for Mumtaz Mahal. It is a miraculous work of marble fulligral work, in laid with semi precious colourful stones. As there are so many jasmine pieces adorned in this tower-hence it is called Jasmine tower also.

It is the death place of Shah Jahan, where he breathed his last in the lap of his dear daughter Jahan Ara gazing towards the Taj, the tomb of his beloved consort.

Nageena Masjid was constructed by Emperor Aurangzeb in 1668 A.D. for the ladies of the Royal Harem. It is situated in the north-west corner or 'Machchi Bhawan' and is of pure white marble. The ladies of the Harem used to perform their prayers in it. Its appearance is small yet it is very beautiful like a gem. There is a door in its southern wall which opens into the 'Meena Bazar'. Diwan-e-Aam, the Hall of Public or Audience was constructed by Akbar the Great with red sand stone and is situated towards the west side of 'Machchi Bhawan'. It was remodeled by Shah Jahan, who built its pillars, arches and ceiling with typical inlayed marble work.

The throne room too was built by Shah Jahan where the Royal Darbar was held to hear the petitioners.

Meena Bazaar was built by Akbar the great for the beautiful ladies of the 'Harem' of Akbar. It was made of red sand stone as a market for selling and purchasing valuable goods by the wives and daughters of the nobles and the chiefs. No male member was allowed to enter in it except the Emperor himself in the disguise so that he may freely enjoy the beauty and charm of this 'Meena Bazaar'. It was organised once in a month and on the the New Year's Day.

Towards the north side of Diwan-l-Aam, there is a beautiful building of white marble is Moti Masjid, built by Emperor Shah Jahan. It had three gates, two to be used by the ladies of the 'Harem' and the one for general public. Its gates are made of red sand stone but two of the gates which were meant for the 'Harem ladies', have been closed. The courtyard of the Mosque is paved with white marble. In the middle of it, there is a small tank. In its south-east corner, there is a marble pillar, which was used to judge the time of offering prayers of 'Namaz'. The interior of this mosque was divided by a row of pillars into three parts. There are two chambers on each side, for the use of the ladies of the 'Harem' and have seating capacity of 90 persons at a time. There are three big domes on the mosque, since some beautiful pearls were hanged in golden chains in the ceiling of it hence it has been named as Pearl-Mosque or 'Moti Masjid'.

Delhi Gate is the main entrance to the fort. This gate faces towards the famous Jama Masjid of Agra. On both the sides of this Delhi Gate, there are two beautifully ornamented towers of white marble. The upper storey of this gate was used as 'Naubat Khana' or Music Hall. On state function and the arrival and on the departure of His Royal Highness the Emperor, the music was played on. On both the sides of this gate, there were two big stone elephants with the statues of two great Rajput fighters or heroes namely Jaimal and Phatte, who fought bravely against Akbar the Great in his battle against Chittor. Though these were enemy warriors yet Akbar honoured them posthumously and 1568 A.D. he made these elephants. That is why this gate was called as Hathi Pole also.

There is a gate situated in the middle of the wall which is in the way of the Yamuna river, this gate is called Water Gate. During the time of Mughals, the flowing waters of the river used to touch the walls of the fort. This gate was the entrance door of the bathing room and was used by the Harem ladies and maids.

(This gate is now closed.)

Chhatrapati Shivaji Maharaja a great king of medieval period, having a great foresight established hindu *swarajya* in the most adverse circumstances, his reign proved to be the best example of welfare administration. His dazzling deeds and courage provided inspiration to those who sought freedom for our country.

Shivaji's growing strength and emperor Aurangzeb immediately realized that Shivaji's *swarajya* can prove to be a threat to the Mughal empire. Shivaji's visited Agra as per Purandar treaty entered into with Mirza Raje Jaisingh. His meeting with Auranzeb took place at Diwan-e-Khas in red fort. In this visit Aurangzeb accorded a humiliating treatment to Shivaji and kept him under house arrest. But with his brave skill and great planning Shivaji successfully managed to escape from this heavily guarded red fort on 17th August 1666 and reached Raigad safely. This is the red fort of Agra where Chhatrapati Shivaji Maharaj was kept under house arrest from 12th may to 17th August 1666.

Apart from these there are many more buildings worth seeing, such as Dakhni Darwaza (South Gate), Baoli, Akbari Mahal, Shahjahani Mahal, Tahkhana, Safed Takht, Kala Takht, Macchi Bhawan, Kursi, Saleem Garh.

C POLICE

ITMAD-UD-DAULAH

Itmad-ud-Daulah is other beautiful historic building in Agra. It is situated on the opposite side of river Jamuna.

It was built by Empress Noor Jahan, the beloved wife of Prince Saleem' or Jahangir, in the memory of her father Mirza Ghiyas Beg, who was the Prime-Minister of the Mughal Court. lt was started in 1622 A.D. and was completed in 1629A.D.

Mirza Ghiyas Beg belonged to a rich family of Tehran, but after the death of his father, fortunes parted from his family and he became poor. He came to Akbar's court for a job and in his way from Tehran to India, Mehr-un-Nisa was born to him. But the poor parents left her in the desert as they were unable to feed her due to extreme poorness. Later on she was picked up by another merchant Mulkniasud, where a snake was guarding her, and was handed over to the poor couple in the way only. They reached Akbar's court at Fatehpur Sikri and Ghiyas Beg was given a job in the Royal court. He rose to a high position of the court and was titled as Munsif Hazari.

The Tomb is of a very peculiar interest as it was the forerunner of the Taj and many of the designs of it were made in the Taj. It is the first building of Mughal Architecture before the existence of the Taj, which was made of white marble. This rectangular shaped tomb of white marble is enclosed by a beautiful garden. The garden is fenced by high walls on three sides and the fourth side opens towards river Jamuna, which gives a beautiful view of the city.

The main entrance gate is made of red sand stone, with a double storied structure which has got inlay work of white marble. Towards its other and towards Jamuna, a beautiful stone Baradary is there. Below this Baradari, there are some rooms which were provided with curtains of Khas-Khas and were used as a cool retreat from the summer heat. The upper chambers were used as bathrooms by the Royal ladies.

It was the first Mughal building, totally constructed of marble and is the first building in which extensive use of 'Pietra dura' has been made, which is characteristic of the Taj. The marble walls are decorated with inscriptions from the holy Quran, cypress trees, vine flasks and jugs carved on marble, are very beautiful. In the centre of the hall are the cenotaphs of Itmad-ud-Daulah and his wife Asmat-ul-Nisa.

The ceiling was decorated with gold and silver, were scrapped away by the Jats during their short occupation of Agra, but were repaired later on by Lord Curzon.

SIKANDRA

Sikandara is one of the superb Mughal buildings, which is situated about 7 km. from Agra city on the Agra-Mathura Road Emperor Akbar the Great selected this place for his burial and started the construction work in 1602 A.D., but it could not be completed as Akbar lived. He was buried here as per his wish in the catacomb. The main building was constructed by Akbar only but was completed by Emperor Jahangir in 1613 A.D. This Mausoleum stands in a big garden called as Bahishtabad in an area of 150 acres, and is enclosed by a huge wall about 25 feet high having 4 gates towards all the four sides.

The gate way of Sikandara is extremely beautiful and is situated on the south side. It is made of red sand stone. Its main door was made of sandal wood, which was taken away by the Jats. Formerly the roof of this gate was decorated with silver and gold which was taken over by the Jats during their short rule. The upper storey of the gate has a 'Naubat Khana', from where the big kettle Drums were played in the morning to evening in the honour of the dead Emperor.

The main building is squarish having four stories and about 100 feet high. The first three stories are of red stone while the fourth one is of white marble, which is a clear evidence that the first three stories of red sandstone were constructed by Akbar, while the fourth one by his son Jahangir. This building has a resemblance with the Panch Mahal of Fatehpur Sikri and both these have a close resemblance of a Buddhist Vihar'.

In the centre of the main building is the grave of Akbar situated on a raised platform, cut out of a single block of marble There is an inscription on the northern side of the cenotaph which reads like this-"Alla-ho-Akbar" (God is Great), and on the south "Jatt-e-Jalal Hoo", (Great is His Glory), and around it there are ninety nine names of 'God or Allah' the Almighty, inscribed in stone.

Near the main gate of Akbar's Tomb towards the south-east side, is a beautiful building called Sheesh-Mahal or the Palace of Mirror. It was constructed by Jahangir for his beloved consort Noor-Jahan. Its beauty is indescribable but its remains are in a dilapidated condition today.

There is another beautiful building towards the west from Akbar's Tomb on Agra Mathura or Delhi Road. It is named as Madam's Tomb or Mariam Zammani's Tomb which was constructed by Jahangir in the memory of his mother Mariam Zammani a title bestowed upon her by Akbar himself. The grave is made of white marble.

"To sum up, this mausoleum is one of the most ambitious productions attempted by the Mughals, yet although a superb effort the result is architecturally ineffective as it lacks substance and volume as well as the qualities of unity and definition."

FATEHPUR SIKRI

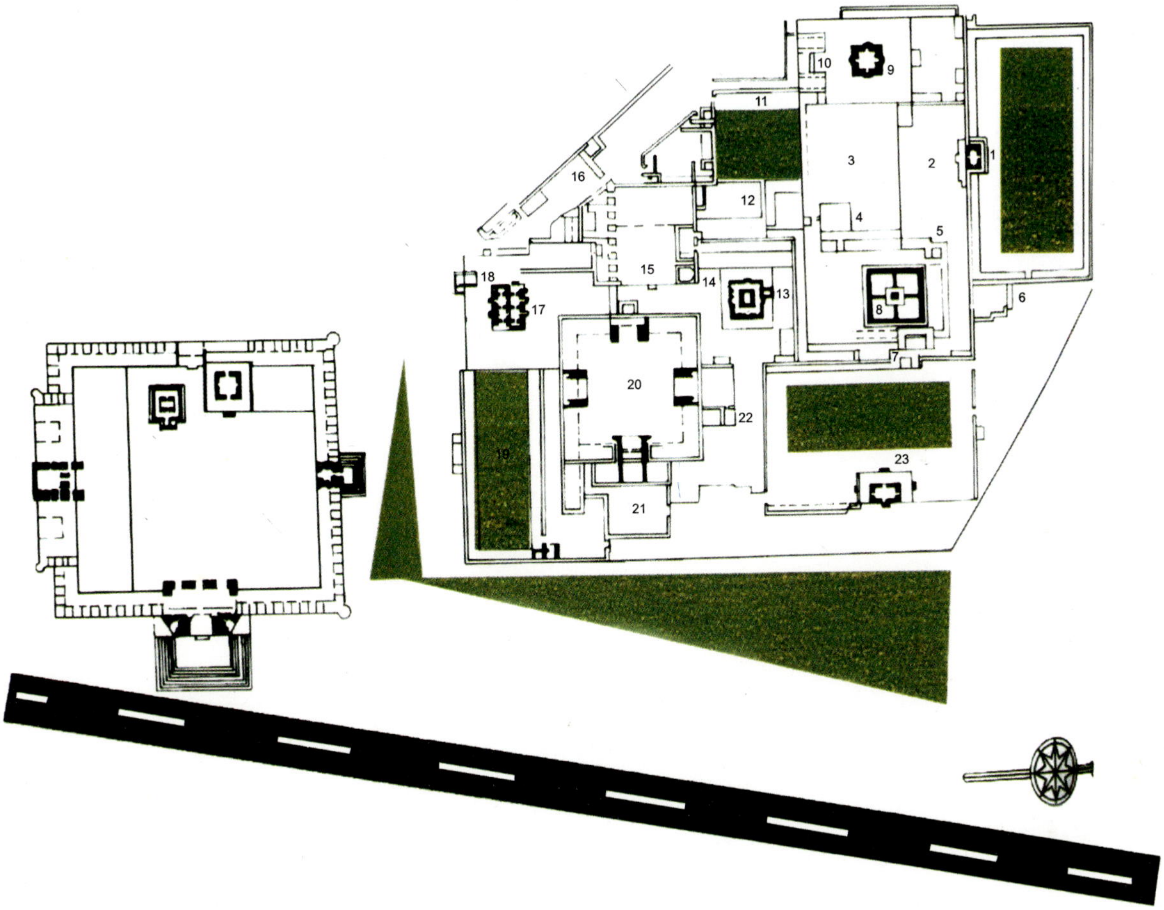

1. Diwan-i-Am (Court of Public audience)
2. Turkish Sultana's Garden
3. Pachisi Court (Court of Games)
4. Girl's School
5. Turkish Sultana's House
6. Turkish Sultana's Bath
7. Khwabagh (Emperor's Sleeping Quarter's)
8. Char Chaman
9. Diwan-i-Khas
10. Anrh Nicbauli (Emperor's Study)
11. Hospital
12. Panch Mahal
13. Mariam's House
14. Mariam's Bath
15. Mariam Garden
16. Nagina Masjid
17. Birbal House
18. Hospital
19. Stables
20. Jodhabai's Palace
21. Bath
22. Guardhouse
23. Daftar Khana
24. Buland Gate
25. Chisti Tomb

FATEHPUR SIKRI

A building having in its centre, a lofty chamber, consisting of a lofty octagonal beautifully carved column. On the top of the pillar is a platform which is enclosed by pierced screen carvings. At all the corners of the platform, there are some kiosks, approachable by two staircases, hewn in the thickness of the walls, the Emperor used to reach his seat by some marble steps, which could be slid beneath the platform. The Emperor used to sit here with his nobles in line, according to their respective ranks. From this place only Akbar used to give' Jaarokha Darshan' to his subjects daily in the morning.

Erected in 1581 the Dargah of Sheikh Salim Chisti is a square building of white marble on the north side of the mosque courtyard. It is a small but very attractive building set up entirely in white marble. It consist of a square exterior of 24 feet side covered by a low dome. It stands on an inlaid marble platform with a portico on the south side considered to be a matchless specimen of marble carving. The pillars are remarkable for their Dravidian character; they are Muhammadan reproduction of a 10th century Siva temple columns. The pillars, particularly those forming the porch are so decorative that they have more the appearance by a verandah closed on the outside by elegant marble screens so rich and delicate in design as to give the effect of lace.

The light is admitted to the central chamber through these screens giving a very soft and subdued effect. The screen is one of the finest specimens of perforated marble work in India and it is remarkable that such large pieces of marble could be worked up into such fascinating patterns without damage.

There is a belief that if an individual wishes for something and ties a thread in the jali around the cenotaph, the wish will surely be fulfilled and if so happens then one has to visit here again and untie the thread.

The exterior walls of the chamber have verses from the Quran inscribed in embossed gilded characters. The whole interior is elaborately decorated in colour and the painted ornamentation is a good example of oriental decoration—the colours are rich and bright. The floor of the chamber and a portion of that of the porch is inlaid in beautiful mosaic in marble.

Buland Darwaza was constructed by Akbar in 1602 A.D. to commemorate

his victory over South India. It is towards the south of the Jama Masjid. It is said to be the grandest and tallest Gate way in India. There are so many stairs steps below this gate which increase its own class, it is one of the greatest doors of the world.

There are some Arabic Texts inscribed on it which after translation reads as follows, " Said Jesuson whom be peace. The world is a bridge, pass over it but build no house. He hopes for an hour hopes for eternity. The world is but an hour spend it in devotion. The rest is unseen." From the top of this gate, the general view of Fatehpur Sikri and a distant view of the Taj can also be enjoyed.

Last but not the least, Agra is not only famous for the beautiful monuments mentioned already, but also for its wide variety of handicrafts, in lay work, carvings on marble, carpets, specially designed cotton durries, leather shoes etc.

The colourful festivals are celebrated with great pomp and show, most famous of them are Sheetla mela, Kailash mela,Taj Mahautsav etc

The cuisine of Agra, includes the famous Mughal food like Biryani, Pulao-rice cooked with meat, nuts and spices., Murgh-e-Musallam-roast chicken etc. Agra is also famous for its delicacies like ganderi and angoori petha and also the dalmoth, which is famous throughout the country.

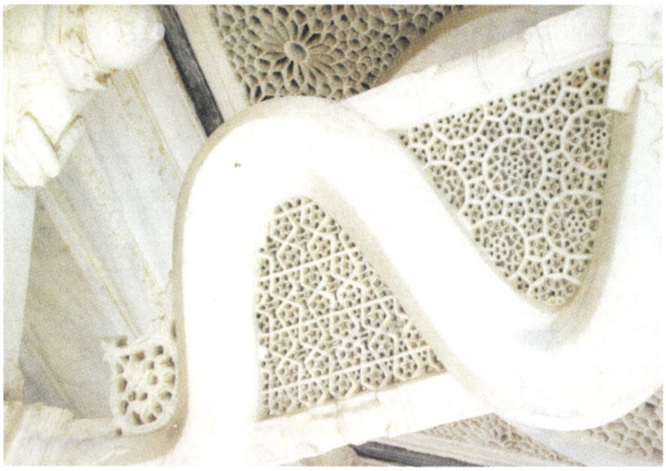

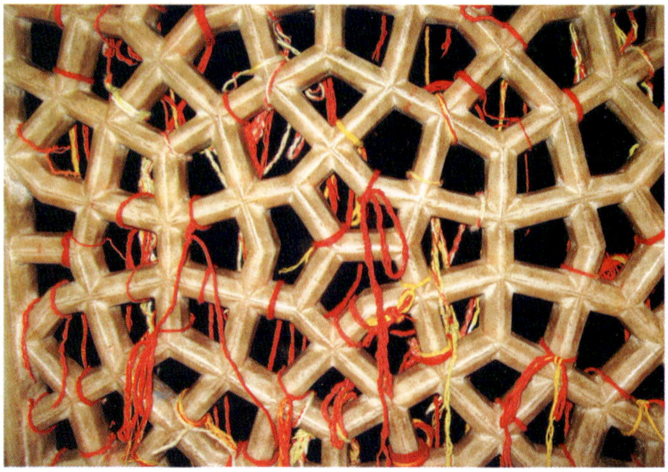